NATURE WATCH
MONKEYS

TOM JACKSON

Consultant: Rachel Hevesi
The Monkey Sanctuary Trust

C O N

Published by Anness Publishing Ltd,
Blaby Road, Wigston,
Leicestershire LE18 4SE

Email: info@anness.com

Web: www.annesspublishing.com

Anness Publishing has a new picture
agency outlet for images for publishing,
promotions or advertising. Please visit our
website www.practicalpictures.com for
more information.

Publisher: Joanna Lorenz
Managing Editor: Linda Fraser
Consultant Editor: Gilly Cameron Cooper
Project Editors: Rebecca Clunes,
Leon Gray
Designer: Caroline Reeves, Aztec Design
Picture Researcher: Veneta Bullen
Illustrator: John Francis
Production Controller: Claire Rae
Editorial Reader: Jonathan Marshall

ETHICAL TRADING POLICY
Because of our ongoing ecological
investment programme, you, as our
customer, can have the pleasure and
reassurance of knowing that a tree is
being cultivated on your behalf to
naturally replace the materials used to
make the book you are holding. For
further information about this scheme,
go to www.annesspublishing.com/trees

TENTS

Prosimians – The First Primates

The earliest primates roamed the world about 25 million years before monkeys evolved. They were the prosimians – which means 'pre-monkeys'. Amazingly, there are still many species of prosimians alive today, including aye-ayes, bush babies, lemurs, lorises and tarsiers.

The prosimians' hands mark them out as primates. They have flexible fingers, and thumbs that work in the opposite direction, making it possible for them to hold and pick things up.

Prosimians rely heavily on their sense of smell to communicate and to find food. The advanced primates – the monkeys and apes – use their sight more. In areas where monkeys and prosimians lived together and competed for the same food, the monkeys were more successful and so prosimians had to develop specialized tactics to survive.

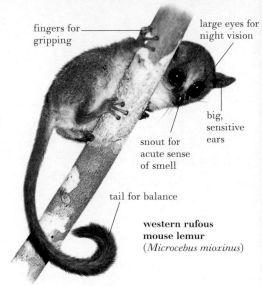

fingers for gripping

large eyes for night vision

big, sensitive ears

snout for acute sense of smell

tail for balance

western rufous mouse lemur
(*Microcebus mioxinus*)

▲ **TYPICAL PROSIMIAN**
This lemur is the smallest primate of all. It weighs only 30g, about the same as a tablespoonful of sugar. Lemurs have characteristics common to all prosimians, but are a distinct group of their own. They live only on the island of Madagascar. Monkeys never crossed the sea to the island once it was cut off from Africa 100 million years ago, so prosimian lemurs survived and evolved into many different species.

EXCLUSIVE OLD WORLDERS ▶
Prosimians live only in parts of Asia and Africa. No species are found in the Americas or in Australia. Bush babies and lorises are found in central and southern Africa. Lemurs live off the east coast of Africa, on the island of Madagascar. The islands and peninsulas of South-east Asia are home to lorises and tarsiers.

North America

Asia

Africa

South America

Australia

Madagascar

◄ USING YOUR EYES

Despite its goggle-eyed appearance, the tarsier from South-east Asia, is more closely related to monkeys than to other prosimians. Most prosimians rely heavily on their sense of smell to communicate and find food. With the tarsier, however, eyesight has become more important. It can swivel its head 180 degrees in each direction to look over its back.

▲ NIGHTWATCH

Bush babies, or galagos, are nocturnal. In daytime, they snuggle up with their family. Some prosimians survived after monkeys evolved by becoming nocturnal and feeding when the monkeys slept. Bush babies live in African forests, feeding on fruit and insects. This South African galago is only about 16cm (a relaxed adult handspan) long, but it can leap up to 5m.

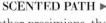

SCENTED PATH ►

Like other prosimians, the slow loris from South-east Asia stakes out its territory with scent. It rubs urine on its hands and feet so that it can imprint its smell exactly where it wants. It also uses the smell to mark its path. The loris moves slowly to avoid attracting attention from predators in the forest. If something frightens it, the loris can easily return to the safety of its nest by following the scented path.

Did you know? Bush babies can grip tightly to a branch for hours without getting tired.

◄ SOCIAL LEMURS

Ring-tailed lemurs are almost as versatile as monkeys. They are agile climbers, and scamper like cats on the ground. They live in large groups, in which females do all the leading and fighting for dominance. Male ring-tailed lemurs fight only over females.

Monkeys Take Over

▲ **DOWN TO EARTH**
Unlike many monkey species, baboons do not live in trees. This olive baboon, which lives in grassland, is typical. Baboons are Old World monkeys, mostly from Africa. They live in large social groups that are among the most complicated and interesting of all monkey societies. All four baboon species are bigger than most monkeys.

In the fierce, overcrowded world of the ancient forests, monkeys had many advantages over prosimians. They had bigger brains and keener eyesight, which enabled them to adapt to different habitats and conditions.

Apes and monkeys evolved around 35 million years ago. At first, apes dominated the forests, but the versatile monkeys soon reigned supreme because they could access foods all over the forest, from the top to the bottom. Because of this, monkeys are still generally built for life in the trees. Most species continue to inhabit warm, wet forests around the Equator, although some have adapted to life on the ground, in desert scrub, on mountains, or even in bustling cities.

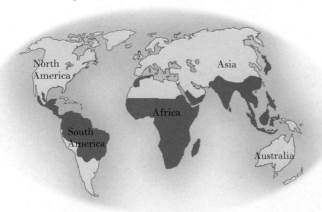

◄ **OLD WORLDS AND NEW**
Monkeys evolved in Africa, and spread to the Americas and Asia. The monkey populations on each side of the ocean developed in different ways. Those that remained in Africa and Asia became known as the Old World monkeys. They evolved into many different species but all have narrow noses and downward-pointing nostrils. The American, or New World, monkeys have wider noses with outward-facing nostrils.

◄ NEW WORLD NOSE STYLE

Like all other monkeys that evolved in the New World, this cotton top tamarin has a flat nose with outward-facing nostrils. New World monkeys live in the forests of Central and South America. Most of them have tails that, unlike those of Old World monkeys, can wrap around and grip on to things, and are used as an extra limb.

tail usually longer than body

forward-facing eyes

long, flexible spine

sitting pads – on Old World monkeys only

WALKING FRAME ►

This Old World monkey from India has many characteristics that are common to all monkeys. Long, slender limbs of about equal length make for easy walking on all fours. Tails are long and flexible – especially on New World monkeys. Hands and feet are designed for climbing, walking on the ground and holding leaves and fruits.

deep, flat chest

long, slender limbs with five-digit hands and feet

hanuman langur
(*Semnopithecus entellus*)

Did you know? Monkeys usually have ridged palms to help them grip on to trees.

OLD WORLD PORTRAIT ►

Look at the downward-pointing, closely spaced nostrils of this pig-tailed macaque. They are typical features of an Old World monkey. These monkeys are more closely related to the great apes such as gorillas and chimpanzees that also live in the Old World. The wide space between lip and nose is typical of many monkeys and apes but unlikely to be seen on prosimians.

7

The Last

One particular group of prosimians flourished in just one place in the world. They were the lemurs of Madagascar. Millions of years ago the island split away from the east coast of Africa, leaving its population of prosimians to evolve separately from those on the mainland. With no competition from monkeys and apes, the lemurs of Madagascar evolved into many different species. Today there are around 40, from the tiny mouse lemur to the athletic sifakas and indris, which are about the weight of a medium-sized monkey. Once people arrived on Madagascar, many species of lemur became extinct, including a huge gorilla-sized lemur.

GHOST DANCE

A sifaka hops daintily over open ground. It spends most of its time leaping athletically through the springy leaves of cactus-like trees. When humans first came to Madagascar, they heard the eerie calls of sifaka troops, glimpsed the white-furred figures and thought that the island was haunted. The animals became known as *lemures* – Latin for 'spirits of the dead'.

ENJOYING THE NIGHTLIFE

The weasel lemur feeds only at night and has a solitary nature, like most of the smaller lemur species. A couple of times a night, a male and female might meet up and groom each other. Most small lemurs eat insects, seeds, gums and fruit. Weasel lemurs, however, are specialist leaf-eaters. Their large intestines break down tough, indigestible plant matter. As an extra aid to digestion and to extract every bit of goodness, they sometimes eat their droppings.

of the *Lemurs*

COOLING OFF

Ring-tailed lemurs bare their chests and splay their legs to lose as much heat as possible in the cool breeze during the day. They are active at night, too, stopping for short breaks every few hours. This helps to keep up their energy levels. These larger lemurs are quite monkey-like in their behaviour. They live in permanent social groups of up to 30, with a female leader. The smaller, nocturnal species tend to lead more solitary lives, like the mainland prosimians.

SOLE SURVIVOR

The aye-aye is the only surviving lemur of its type, and is itself threatened with extinction. It has survived as long as this by being highly specialized – a long middle finger with a claw-like nail hooks out grubs from wood, or the pulp from fruit, as in this picture. Aye-ayes are very secretive and move about only at night. During the day, they curl up in a nest of leaves.

HIGH-LEVEL LIVING

Ruffed lemurs rarely touch the ground. Their short legs are more suited to running and jumping through the trees than to climbing like the longer-limbed sifakas and indris. As they eat more fruit than other lemurs, they do a useful job of spreading seeds via their droppings. All lemurs, and the ruffed lemur in particular, have a snout like that of a wild dog. This provides more surface area for picking up smells.

Outward Appearances

Monkeys and prosimians became experts in forest survival. As different species evolved, each adapting to a particular way of life, a great variety of shapes and sizes emerged. All, however, had the primate speciality of flexible hands and fingers. Thumbs work in the opposite direction to the fingers so that the digits can close together and grasp. Long arms and legs are geared for climbing. On many species the arms and legs are of similar length – which means the animals can walk comfortably on all fours. On others, strong hind legs provide power for leaping. These primates can stand or sit on their haunches, leaving both hands free.

▲ **UNDER THE THUMB**
The pygmy marmoset from South America is small enough to fit on the palm of your hand. It is only about 30cm from its head to the tip of its tail, and weighs about 100g – 500 times less than a mandrill.

▼ **BIG AND BULKY**
Male mandrills are the world's biggest monkeys. They weigh 50kg, about the same as a small adult human. Mandrills walk on all fours and have limbs of roughly the same length. They do not live in trees so they don't need a tail.

▲ **THE FIFTH LIMB**
A black-handed spider monkey has a muscular tail that can wrap around a branch. A hairless stretch of ridged skin on the underside gives extra grip, like the ridges on the palm of a primate hand. Only New World monkeys have tails with this prehensile (grasping) power. The tails of prosimians and Old World monkeys simply help to balance them when leaping through the trees.

▲ HANDS ON

The long, flexible fingers of the tarsier are padded for extra grip when climbing. The tarsier is a prosimian from South-east Asia. As with almost all primates, it has fingernails. For animals that forage for plant food, fingernails are more useful than claws. They can be used for picking, peeling and gouging as well as for scratching and grooming.

▲ GETTING A GRIP

A young vervet makes the most of its hands and feet to climb. Its opposing thumbs curve in to help it grip. Balanced securely on two feet and one hand, the monkey has one hand free for eating. Monkey hands need to hold small items, so tend to be smaller and more flexible than their feet.

◄ PROBLEM HAIR AND SKIN

A rhesus macaque pulls ticks from her friend. The fur of monkeys is home to many tiny insects that suck the host's blood or make the skin flaky. Monkeys deal with the problem by grooming each other. Grooming is also an important way of making friends. Monkey skin darkens with age because of the effects of sunlight and so many monkeys avoid spending too much time in the sun.

A HANDY FUR COAT ►

For a new-born chacma baboon, mother's fur is handy to cling on to. In the sun-baked savannas, baboons do not need to keep warm, so the baby's fur will become coarse and sparse like its mother's. Fur also gives some necessary protection against the burning sun, and its grey-brown colour provides good camouflage on the African plains.

Inner Power

In terms of brainpower, monkeys and other primates are often considered more 'advanced' than other animals. Their bodies, however, are basically the same as most other mammals. Primates did not develop special physical features like animals that grew hooves or horns.

Small primate bodies are built for flexibility and agility, with hinged joints supported by long, elastic muscles to allow maximum range of movement. Different species have body shapes adapted to whether they climb and leap through trees, or move along the ground. Head shape and size depend on whether brainpower or the sense of smell or sight is top priority. Digestive systems vary according to diet.

▲ **DENTAL PRACTICE**
Monkeys and prosimians have four types of teeth. There are incisors for cutting, canines for stabbing and ripping, and molars and premolars for grinding tough leaves and fruit into a mushy paste.

▼ **INTERNAL VIEW**
A monkey's bones and strong muscles protect the vital organs inside its body. Its facial muscles allow it to make expressions. Monkey legs are generally shorter in relation to their bodies than prosimian legs. This gives them more precise climbing and reaching skills, especially in the treetops.

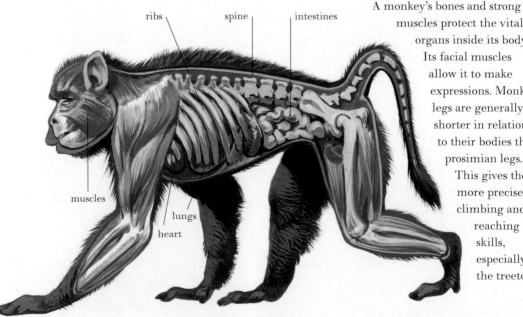

ribs　　spine　　intestines

muscles

lungs

heart

▼ BIG EYES

The tarsier has the biggest eyes of any animal in relation to its body size. There is not much room left in its skull for a brain and each of the eyes is heavier than the brain. Prosimians have simpler lives than monkeys and do not need big brains. Instead, they have an array of sharp senses – more sensitive than a monkey's – that help them to survive. As well as its huge eyes, this tarsier has large ears that pick up the slightest sounds in the quiet of the night.

▲ A STRONG STOMACH

A baboon's digestive system can cope with raw meat as well as plant food. Although meat is nutritious, it can be harmful if it stays in the body too long. Meat-eaters have shorter guts than vegetarians, so that food passes through the body quickly. Most monkeys and prosimians eat mainly plants and have longer guts because leaves and other plant foods are hard to digest.

INSIDE LOOK AT A LEMUR ▶

The skeleton of this prosimian, a ruffed lemur, is quite different from that of a monkey. It has a long, narrow head, which has less space for the brain, and its legs are very long compared to the length of its body. Their long legs help lemurs to leap great distances from tree to tree. Because their legs and feet are designed for climbing, they can also cling in a relaxed fashion to sheer, upright tree trunks.

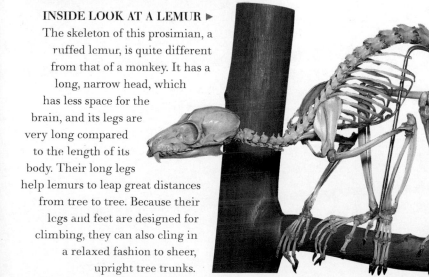

13

Sensing the Surroundings

Monkeys are usually active in the daytime, and make the most of their excellent colour vision. Most prosimians are nocturnal, and have eyes to help them see at night. The eyes of all primates are lined with a combination of cone cells and rod cells. Monkeys have more colour-sensitive cone cells. Prosimians have plenty of rod cells, designed to see in dim light. Their eyes glow in the dark like cats' eyes because they are backed by a mirror-like layer that reflects every bit of available light.

Sight is very important to monkeys, but prosimians rely much more on the senses of smell and hearing. The ears of prosimians are constantly on the alert. The slightest rustle in the dark could identify an insect snack or an approaching predator.

▲ COLOUR SELECTION
Thanks to its colour vision, an African vervet monkey can select its favourite flowers when they are at the peak of perfection. Many leaf-eating monkeys have eyes that are particularly sensitive to different shades of green. This means that they can easily identify the fresh green of tender young leaves which are good to eat.

MIDNIGHT MONKEY ▶
Douracouli monkeys are the only nocturnal monkeys. They live in South America where there are no prosimians to compete with. Like prosimians, their eyes are big to catch maximum light. They are able to pick up detail but not colour.

▲ EYES LIKE SAUCERS
Unlike the eyes of many prosimians, tarsier's eyes have no reflective layer, but their size means they catch as much light as possible. Like monkeys, their eyes have a sensitive area called the fovea, which picks out very sharp detail.

▼ A KEEN SENSE OF SMELL

An emperor tamarin monkey marks its territory with scent. New World monkeys and prosimians have a smelling organ in the roof of their mouths that Old World monkeys do not have. They use their sense of smell to communicate with each other and to identify food that is good and ready to eat.

▲ WET NOSED SMELLING AIDS

Look at the shiny nose of this ruffed lemur. It is more like that of a cat or dog than a monkey. Most prosimians have this moist nostril and lip area, called the rhinarium. It gives them a better sense of smell. The nose has a layer of sensitive cells to detect chemicals in the air. The cells work better when they are wet.

▼ MUFFLED SENSE OF HEARING

The furry ears of squirrel monkeys probably muffle sound. But although these and other monkeys use sound to communicate with each other, hearing is not as important for them as keen eyesight. Nocturnal primates, however, have highly sensitive, delicate-skinned ears.

On the Move

Primates are the most versatile movers of the animal world. Many can walk and run, climb and swim. Small monkeys and the larger lemurs can leap between branches. This method is risky for larger animals, in case a branch breaks beneath their weight. Heavier primates play safe by walking along branches on all fours and avoid jumping if possible.

When branches are bendy, climbers move with caution. They may use their weight to swing from one handhold to the next, but they do not let go of one handhold until the other is in place.

Did you know? A spider monkey's tail is so strong it can support the monkey's entire weight.

◀ CLIMBING POWER

New World monkeys rarely move at ground level. They swing from tree to tree, stop and whip their tail around a branch, let go with both hands and grab something to eat. Old World monkeys do not have a prehensile (grasping) tail. Many have lost their tails altogether or have very short ones, which they use to help balance in the trees.

◀ PADDED MITTS

The palm of a sifaka lemur is just one of the features that makes it a star jumper. The wrinkles and flesh pads are like a baseball glove, giving extra holding power. Sifakas can push off from their long hind legs to leap up to 5m high. Their arms are short, making it impossible to walk on all fours. Instead, sifakas hop on both feet.

◀ BABOONS ON THE MOVE

A troop of baboons makes its way down a track in the African savanna. They are strong and tough because they have to walk long distances to find enough food to feed the troop. Baboons and other monkeys that walk on the ground, such as mandrills, geladas and macaques, put their weight on the fingertips and palms of their hands and feet. This is different from apes, such as gorillas and chimpanzees, who walk on their knuckles.

▲ SLENDER LORIS

Lorises from Sri Lanka and southern India are known for their slow, deliberate movements. They have long, thin arms and legs with very flexible ankles and wrists. A loris can wriggle its way through and get a grip on dense twigs and small branches. Due to its strange appearance, some people describe the animal as a banana on stilts.

LIGHT AS AIR ▶

A pygmy marmoset can perch on the flimsiest of twigs. It has to be small, light and quick so that it can catch insects to eat. Marmosets scurry along branches rather like squirrels, and for this reason are the only primates to have claws instead of nails. They are also able to sit up on their hind legs to free their hands for collecting food as well as for feeding.

17

The Fast,

Long limbs, strong back muscles and a super-long tail make langurs the supreme all-round athletes of the monkey world. They are masters of balance, suspension and speed; as agile on the ground as at the very top of a forest canopy. They can leap farther than most other monkeys, and spend up to 70 per cent of their time moving around the trees.

Langurs live in big troops in south Asian countries, such as Bangladesh, India and Bhutan. The males in a troop try bossing the females around, but the females are really in charge of everything apart from mating. The females also help each other out by sharing childcare.

COMING TO GROUND

A golden langur sits and waits for other members of the troop. Gatherings usually occur in the mornings. They take place on or close to the ground, as there is more space than in the trees.

CLING ON

Long limbs make langurs great at rope-climbing – or in this case climbing a liana (trailing plant). Where trees are more spaced out, langurs are happy to move at ground level. If danger arises, they can speed overland at around 40km/hour.

BALANCING ACT

A langur reaches out to grab some flowers. The branch sways precariously, but the langur is perfectly balanced. Its heavy tail hangs like a plumb weight beneath to secure its position. Langurs have a vegetarian diet of fruits, flowers, berries, shoots and leaves.

Acrobatic Langurs

WELL SPOTTED

Juicy fruit on a neighbouring tree has caught this golden langur's eye. A super-sensitive patch on each retina enables it to focus sharply. The langur's vision also helps it to measure distances for leaping. Their eyes are almost identical in strength and ability to human eyes.

LEAPING FROM TREE TO TREE

As they fly from one tree to another, langurs whoop to other members of the troop to follow. They can leap or drop a dizzying 20m – the height of a two-storey house. Brainpower combined with learning when young, by watching older members of the troop, mean that the monkeys judge distances very accurately.

TIGHTROPE WALKING

A langur walks along a long branch on its hands and feet in the same way it would if it was on solid ground. The monkeys find it easy to do this because they spend so much of their time in the trees.

Brainpower

To survive in the complicated world of forest branches, monkeys developed intelligence. They have excellent hand–eye co-ordination to make the most of their grasping hands and forward-facing eyes. In the forest, monkeys move fast and make split-second decisions such as: "Will that branch hold my weight?" They can work out what the likely effect of their actions might be.

As they live in groups, monkeys have developed their brainpower so that they can negotiate with each other. Another skill for group living is a good memory, and monkeys are certainly good at remembering things. They rely on their memory to identify areas where they found last year's choicest food supplies.

◄ **PROSIMIAN TEAM**
Prosimians that are active in the day, such as these ring-tailed lemurs, are usually cleverer than nocturnal prosimians. Like monkeys, they live in groups and have to work together to control territory and find food.

▼ **THE EVIDENCE FOR INTELLIGENCE**
The skull of a sifaka (*below*) has little brain space, even though it is probably the most intelligent prosimian. The brain makes up less than half the length of the sifaka's skull.

The front section – the nose – is long, which reflects the importance of the sifaka's sense of smell. The vervet monkey skull (*right*) is a different shape, with a much larger area behind its eye sockets for the brain.

Monkey Dance
In Mexico, people dress up as monkeys for some traditional dances. The Mayans believed that when the world began, monkeys were types of humans. The monkeys fled to live high in trees because they were tired of being laughed at by other humans.

▲ FINE JUDGEMENT

Thanks to its large brain, this red colobus monkey can make death-defying leaps with absolute precision. Even on jumps of over 20m – the length of a tennis court – it can work out that the jump is possible and where to land safely. The monkey's sense of sight is also vital for gauging the distance between take-off and landing.

▲ LOOK AND LEARN

Toque macaques probably learned to raid rubbish bins for food by watching humans. Their big monkey brains give them the capacity to learn. This ability to learn means that monkeys can adapt to new environments. Macaques have worked out how to survive in a greater variety of habitats than any other monkey.

▲ SOCIAL CONSCIENCE

The members of this troop of chacma baboons all know each other very well. Because they are intelligent, each baboon can remember how other baboons have behaved and reacted in the past. As a result some are good friends, while others are not so close. Some baboons are even enemies. A monkey's intelligence means that it can live in complicated societies like this.

▲ LIMITED NEEDS, SMALL BRAIN

Most prosimians do not need to move and think quickly. They do not have the stimulation of group living, so they do not need as big a brain as a monkey.

Changing Habitats

Nearly all monkeys and prosimians live in steamy rainforests, like their early ancestors. Many monkeys may never touch the ground. Some live right at the top of the tallest trees, leaping from branch to branch. Others live lower down, where branches are so thick that they form an almost solid platform. Species that live in the forest understorey are agile both on the ground and in the trees.

Ground-based baboons and monkeys evolved later than the forest-dwellers. Sometimes, they live far from forests. There are fewer species and smaller social groups in open areas than in the forest, as food is more scarce.

▲ GROUND-BASED

Gelada baboons come from the open grasslands in the Ethiopian highlands in Africa. They are the only monkeys that eat mostly grass, and they live in groups for safety from predators. Like other ground-based monkeys, they have stout bodies for walking long distances in search of food.

Did you know? Some females don't eat in the dry season, living off the fat they store in their tails.

EXTREME VERSATILITY ▶

A Tibetan macaque has a thick winter coat and must rest more than other monkeys to save energy for keeping warm. It gets very cold high in the mountains and food is scarce. The macaques grow thick winter coats to trap heat. Macaques are among the most adaptable of monkeys. Different species have learned to survive farther north than any other monkey, in mountain forests and in cities.

in the Snow

4 A snow monkey eats bark stripped from a tree. It will also feed on tree buds and seeds if it can find any. In the very coldest areas, snow monkeys only find about half the food they need to stay alive in the winter months. The rest of the nutrition their bodies need comes from fat stores built up during the previous summer.

6 Japanese macaques cannot sleep in the water, so they have to get out when they are tired. To stay warm the monkeys huddle into large groups. Together, their bodies lose heat more slowly during the icy nights. Long hairs on the outside of the monkeys' coats prevent snow from reaching their skin and keeps them dry.

5 One of the ways in which snow monkeys are able to survive the extreme cold is by having a hot bath. Some years ago, scientists observed a few monkeys taking a trial bath in a hot volcanic spring. Others in the troop followed suit, and now it is a regular snow monkey habit. Because they are using less energy to stay warm, they are conserving vital stores of fat.

Diets for Living

Very few small primates eat just one type of food. Most eat whatever's available through the seasons. Some species, such as mandrills and baboons, range over a wide territory to find enough food to feed the troop. Some become specialists, such as the leaf-eating colobus monkeys of Africa and Asia. They have sharp molar teeth to chop the leaves finely, and extra-big stomachs to extract as much goodness as possible from the tough fibres. Most monkeys eat a varied diet of fruit, nuts and insects, and a few eat eggs and small animals. In general, small monkeys eat more high-energy foods than larger monkeys because they burn up energy faster and need more efficient fuel.

▲ CLEAN FOOD

A Japanese macaque washes meat before eating it. It does not understand that unclean meat may make it ill, but knows that dirt spoils the taste. Once one monkey started to wash food, others in the group copied it. The habit will be passed on to their children. Other troops have not learned to do this.

▲ LAID-BACK EATERS

Red colobus monkeys usually eat leaves, although they also like flowers and fruits. Colobus monkeys do not need to look far for food as leaves are plentiful. They spend a long time sitting still, digesting the leaves to make the most of the limited goodness in them.

▲ SAP EXTRACTION

A bare-faced tamarin licks the thick, sweet juice from a fruit. Tamarins and their marmoset cousins eat a lot of resin from trees, including liquid rubber. Marmosets have pointed bottom teeth with which they pierce the bark so that the liquid flows out.

Greedy Monkey

A fable from Pakistan tells of a monkey that found some wheat inside a small hollow in a rock. The monkey thrust in its hand and filled it with the grain. The opening was too narrow for it to pull out its hand without letting go of some of the food. The monkey was too greedy to let go of any of the food, with the result that it had no food at all.

▲ BABOON ATTACK

A male olive baboon normally eats seeds, insects and grasses, but will not refuse the carcass of a baby animal. This African antelope fell victim to a baboon troop. The monkeys edge towards a herd until a young, weak animal is isolated. Then they rip it to shreds.

▼ SAVING FOR LATER

A drill has filled its cheek pouches with chewed food. Some other Old World monkeys do this too. They do this when they are eating leaves so that chemicals in the monkeys' spit begin to break the leaves down. The monkey's stomach will be able to absorb the nutrients more easily from the resulting mush.

▲ EAT UP YOUR PETALS

Flowers are a good supply of food, as this ring-tailed lemur is discovering. The pollen has a higher concentration of protein than any other part of the plant. Many insects are also attracted to flowers, and they are another good source of protein for monkeys and prosimians.

27

Sharing Space

When monkeys evolved, many prosimians became extinct, because the two groups of animals were competing for the same food. One way to survive in such circumstances is to become a specialist in a particular environment. Gradually, different species of monkeys and prosimians evolved that were able to share space in the same patch of forest. They had different diets, ate at different times, or operated at different levels in the trees.

Monkeys also share the forest with many other animals and plants. Together they make up an ecosystem. If an imbalance occurs in any part of the ecosystem, everything is affected. Too many leaf-eating monkeys living in one area, for example, might strip a tree of its leaves. The tree, and all the insects that rely on it then die, and the leaf-eaters, as well as any insect-eating monkeys, lose their food supply.

◄ MY PATCH!

All species of the South American dusky titi monkey eat seeds and fruits. Each one, though, feeds at a different level of the forest. They do not compete with each other, but may be chased from food by larger monkeys. When this happens, dusky titis switch to eating leaves.

◄ OPPORTUNISTS

Baboons are the only monkeys to live on the dry, open grasslands of Africa. They have adapted to eating anything they can find – even grass. The monkeys share the savanna with grazing animals such as wildebeest. There are no other monkeys here as there is not enough food. Even the baboons have to walk a long way each day to find enough to eat.

▲ SECURITY SERVICE

This pig-like animal is a peccary from South America. Peccaries are often found living close to monkeys, to the benefit of both. The hogs root around the bases of trees, feeding on insects, roots and whatever monkeys may drop from the branches. In return, peccaries will attack snakes heading up the trunk, which may be after small monkeys.

▲ MIDNIGHT FEAST

Night monkeys live in the same parts of the South American forest as other types of monkey. They eat many of the same foods, but feed at night, so do not compete. In the same way, nocturnal prosimians can hold their own against monkeys in the same forest.

SPECIALIST LEAF-EATER ▶

A black howler monkey feeds on its main diet of leaves in the South American rainforest. As the only leaf-eaters, troops of howlers can share space with fruit or insect-eating monkeys. However, other monkeys tend to give the large, noisy howlers a wide berth.

▼ MILITARY TACTICS

Sharing space means developing self-protection. Baboon troops move in a defensive column with the largest males at the front and back. Females walk in the centre with their young. When a predator, such as this leopard, attacks, the males rush forward to fight off the big cat. The females gather with the young baboons at a safe distance.

Territorial Rights

Troops of monkeys spend their lives in one clearly defined area. They create mental maps of their territories, knowing exactly where seasonal food supplies are, for example. Monkeys and social prosimians, such as sifakas and ring-tailed lemurs, defend their territory from neighbouring bands. These group-living primates mark their territory with scent and fiercely defend it against rivals of the same species who may be looking for more space or better food.

Small nocturnal prosimians live solitary lives and do not worry when a neighbour crosses their patch. They are more likely to mate with it or even ignore it altogether.

A primate's territory varies in size according to how many other animals there are and on food supply. A rainforest rich in food can support many animals in small territories. On the plains, animals need to range over a wide area to find enough food.

▲ CALLING CARD
The female leader of a troop of ring-tailed lemurs from Madagascar marks her territory with scent from a gland on her chest. In ring-tailed lemur society, it is the females who fight to defend territory. Males only fight over females.

◄ FOREST RANGERS
Squirrel monkeys live in large societies of up to 50 members. Groups move around a home range of 20km², but territorial boundaries are blurred. One troop may merge with another without a hint of a fight. These bands of monkeys have no permanent troops, leaders or clearly defined territories. They roam through the South American forest looking for fruit, and keeping track of each other by high-pitched calling.

◄ ON THE MOVE

Baboons live on the African savanna where food supplies are very spread out. They live in big troops of up to 150 animals. This gives them the power to defend massive territories of 40km². The monkeys walk about 5km each day to collect enough food for the troop. Most other monkeys move through only a few trees each day.

UNITED WE STAND ►

Langurs live in large troops that are controlled by a single male. They patrol big home ranges throughout India, but do not live in rainforests. The troop's leader is always wary of attack from rival males wishing to steal his females and land. The whole langur troop may become involved in a battle with neighbouring troops for control of territory.

◄ KEEP OFF MY LAND

A howler monkey gives a loud, roaring howl warning other troops to keep out of their territory. Both males and females make this noise, and fight off invaders. In the thick forest, sound is a more effective way to assert territorial rights than scent. Fiercely defensive species, such as howler and proboscis monkeys, are the noisiest monkeys of all. The males are the most aggressive, as they also fight for the right to mate with females.

31

Trumpeters of

LAZY DAYS
This family group of proboscis monkeys spends most of its day eating, high in the trees. They do take time off, though, to groom and to play with each other.

If you are a male proboscis monkey, the larger and more bulbous your nose, the better. It makes you look more fearsome to a rival male and it impresses the females. Most importantly, it swells the volume of your territorial honking sounds.

A single dominant male proboscis monkey controls a group of several females and their young. Bachelor males live in separate bands. They all make a lot of noise, screaming, growling and shrieking to each other.

The monkeys spend most of their time in the upper branches, feeding on various leaves, fruits and seeds.

THE PROTECTOR
A male takes up a prominent position to watch out for rival males who may try to steal his harem. Male proboscis monkeys are nearly twice the size of females so that they can look as tough as possible to other males.

SAFE AND SOUND
Females do not defend territory or fight. They have smaller prosbosces (noses). Newborn babies have bright blue faces to alert other members of the troop to look after them. As they grow up and fend for themselves, their faces take on adult colours.

the Swamps

LOUD AND CLEAR

An adult male honks loudly to announce his territorial rights. Inside the enormous nose are hollow spaces that act like loudspeakers. As he honks, his proboscis (nose) straightens and stiffens. The sound echoes around the spaces and is amplified (made louder) so that it travels farther through the forest. The males also honk to frighten away predators, and snort to keep the family group in order.

DANGEROUS CROSSING

A proboscis monkey makes a solo voyage through water. Proboscis monkeys have to be very good swimmers because their territory is laced with rivers and inlets. They cross at the narrowest possible point, one at a time, then if a gharial (a type of small crocodile) strikes, it will get only one monkey. It is safer still to find a suitable tree with bouncy branches that the monkeys can use as a springboard to jump across the water.

NOWHERE TO GO

The proboscis monkey's home in the mangrove swamps of Borneo in South-east Asia is being taken over by roads and towns. Many troops are trapped in small islands of mangrove forest with territories too small for their needs. In addition, the coastal plants contain minerals that the monkeys need to stay alive. They cannot survive on similar food that grows inland. Many starve to death.

Predator and Victim

Danger is a way of life for small primates. One false move for a tree-living monkey could mean a long fall to its death on the forest floor. There are hungry predators, too, waiting for a tasty prosimian or monkey.

Small primates that move in the upper branches are in a good position to see any predators approaching from the ground and have plenty of time to move away. However, they are at greater risk from attack by birds of prey, such as eagles. Living in the middle branches offers protection from attack by air and from many ground predators, but tree snakes are a threat. They may spend days waiting motionless for prey to pass close by before striking. Prosimians that shuffle along at ground level by night are in danger from wild cats, silent snakes and swooping owls.

▲ **EAGLE-EYES**
Harpy eagles can swoop between tree branches to grab prey. The South American eagles make nests high in dead, leafless trees. From this exposed position, they watch for food such as monkeys, sloths and birds.

◄ **DANGEROUS CROSSINGS**
In the rivers and lakes of the African grasslands, crocodiles often lie in wait for prey to come near the water. They may snap up a few baboons as troops cross rivers in their quest for food. Swamp monkeys, crab-eating macaques and capuchins spend a lot of time near water and they, too, provide welcome snacks for various local species of crocodiles.

▲ SNAKE IN THE GRASS

A python squeezes the life out of a grey langur monkey. Snakes are a danger to monkeys both on the ground and in the trees. Some snakes squeeze their prey to death, others inject fast-acting venom to kill. Tree-living snakes hold on to their prey as it dies to prevent it from falling out of the branches.

▲ GANG WARFARE

In the African jungle, chimpanzees form hunting parties to attack monkeys such as red colobuses. The monkeys are light and agile, but the chimps are clever and work as a team. One chimp separates a couple of monkeys from the colobus troop and drives them through the forest. Other chimps are stationed nearby to block any escape routes. Chasers force the victims into an ambush, where an old, experienced chimp lies in wait, ready to pounce. Victims are ripped apart in a matter of minutes, and the meat is shared out among the adult chimpanzees in order of importance.

LONE HUNTER ▶

A leopard holds a young baboon in its massive jaws. These predators of the African plains hunt alone. They use stealth to catch their prey off guard, preferring to attack at dusk or at night. The cat often quietly positions itself in a tree or high on some rocks and leaps down on to its prey from above. It will then drag its meal back to the vantage point, where it can eat in peace.

Living Together

All primates communicate in some way with other members of their species, and most of them live in social groups. Community living has advantages. There are more eyes to spot predators, and several animals can work as a team to fight off attack or forage for food. As a community, they stand a better chance of survival if there is a problem with the food supply, during a drought, for instance. The leaders will feed themselves and their young first to make sure that they survive. Solitary animals may have a hard time finding a mate, but within a group, there's plenty of choice. And, when there are young to be cared for, a community can provide many willing helpers.

Nocturnal prosimians rely on being solitary and silent to avoid being noticed by predators. Among bush babies and lorises, even couples live independently of each other, but they occupy the same patch, and their paths often cross. Babies stay with their mother until they are old enough to live alone.

▲ TREE-SHARING
Sifakas work together in groups of about seven adults to defend their territory. They are generally led by the females, and males may swap between groups. These prosimians gather in the higher branches of the trees in western Madagascar. If danger threatens, they all start a hiccuping groan.

HAPPY COUPLE ▶
In the jungles of South America, male and female sakis mate and usually live as a couple for a year. The female cares for the young. The father may not spend the day with his family, but does return to them at night. If there is plenty of food, families mingle with each other, forming large, loosely-knit groups.

◄ FEMALE RULE

A female is in charge of this troop of black tufted-ear marmosets. As with most other New World marmosets and tamarins, there may be several other females, but only the head female breeds. She mates with all the males to make sure her top-level genes are passed on. As none of the males knows who is the father, they all help rear and protect the young.

EQUAL SOCIETY ►

The relationship between a woolly monkey mother and her children can last for life. Woolly monkeys live in troops — there may be 20 to 50 of them in each group, with roughly equal numbers of males and females. Adult males often cooperate, and all the males and females can mate with each other. Individual females care for their own young. Woolly monkey groups are bound by an intricate web of relationships between all members that is hard for outsiders to understand.

◄ MALE POWER

These female hamadryas baboons are just two in a harem of several females. One top male mates with all the females to make sure he fathers all the children. Males with no harem live in separate bachelor groups of two or three. They try to mate with a member of the harem when the leader is not looking. When the leader gets old, a few young males will team up to depose him. Once he has been chased away, the victors fight for control of the harem.

37

Communication

Attracting attention in a noisy forest is a challenge. Groups of tree-living monkeys and prosimians lose sight of each other and keep in touch by calling. Nocturnal prosimians, however, need to keep a low profile, and so they leave scent messages that are easier to place accurately.

All prosimians and, to a lesser extent, monkeys, send messages of ownership, aggression or sexual readiness with strong-smelling urine, or scent from special glands. Monkeys can also express their feelings with facial expressions and gestures, and some use their ability to see in colour. African guenons, for example, have brightly coloured patches on their bodies that can be seen by their companions when they are hurtling through the trees. Even fur and tails can be useful. Ring-tailed lemurs swish their tails menacingly at rivals, and at the same time, fan evil smells over them.

▲ DON'T HURT ME
This toque macaque is showing by its posture and expression that it is no threat. If an adult monkey wants to make friends, it may make a sound like a human baby gurgling. The other monkey will usually respond gently.

Did you know? Monkeys have more face muscles than prosimians and pull more expressions.

PERSONAL PERFUME ▶
A black spider monkey smears a strong-smelling liquid on a branch. The liquid is produced by a gland on the monkey's chest. Its smell is unique to this monkey. When other monkeys smell it, they know that another of their kind has been there. If they meet the particular monkey that left the scent, they will recognize it.

◄ TELL-TAIL SIGNS

In complicated langur societies, high-ranking males hold their tails higher than lesser members of the group. Primates that live in complex social groups have a wider range of communication skills than solitary species. More information has to be passed around among a greater number of individuals.

▲ YOU SCRATCH MY BACK...

Grooming a fellow monkey not only gets rid of irritating fleas and ticks, but also forges a relationship. A lot of monkey communication is about preventing conflicts among group members. Forming strong personal bonds hold the troop together.

▲ BE CAREFUL

A mandrill has mobile face muscles to make different expressions. Here, he pulls back his gums and snarls. This makes him look very menacing to other males.

▲ I'M ANGRY

When a mandrill becomes angry, he opens his mouth in a wide yawn to show the size of his teeth and roars. Another monkey will hesitate before confronting this male.

LOOKING FIERCE ►

This marmoset is literally bristling for a fight. Its fur stands on end like an angry cat's to make it look much bigger. It may scare its rival into withdrawing. Marmosets look cute, but they squabble a lot among themselves.

Bright Colours

The startling colours of the male mandrill's face and rump make practical sense. They act like beacons in the gloom of the dense tropical forests of Central Africa. Troops of mandrills roam over large territories of around 50km², so they need to stay in touch with each other.

Groups of about 20 monkeys, made up of a ruling male, several females and more lowly males, may join forces to make armies of up to 250 or more. The monkeys are strongly built with limbs of equal length for moving around at ground level. At night, they climb into the lower branches of trees to sleep.

LIGHT SNACK
A mandrill spends much of its day rooting for food such as fruit, seeds, or sometimes bird's eggs and small animals. The troop breaks up into small foraging parties to feed.

LOOKING COOL
You can tell that this male is in a relaxed mood, because his colours are quite muted. If he becomes agitated, though, the colours on his broad and boney muzzle flare up. Mandrills are the largest monkeys. The male weighs about 50kg – about the same as a small woman.

MODESTY MOST OF THE TIME
Female mandrills are about half the size of the males, and duller in colour. When ready to mate, a female sends out a colour signal. Her bottom swells and turns bright red. Females have one baby at a time. Other members of the troop may help find food for a nursing mother.

of the Mandrills

FOLLOW THE LEADER

All male mandrills have bottoms covered in blue, purple and red skin, with no long tail to reduce the impact of the strong colours. This makes sense in a dark forest, where it is easy to lose the way. Mandrill troops simply spot and follow the colourful male bottoms in front of them. The leading mandrill has the most vividly coloured rump. He also decides when to eat, and when to move on. He grunts to announce to the other monkeys when time is up.

BIG TEETH

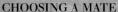

The male mandrill's vampire-like canine teeth, which are around 6cm long, are nothing to do with its eating habits. Instead they are used as fearsome weapons during fights. The males of a troop of mandrills are constantly fighting to improve their rank because the top male is the only one who gets to mate with all the females.

CHOOSING A MATE

Female mandrills want their children to be as healthy as possible, so when they look for a mate, they choose a strong male leader. A male's large size and quality of colour are signs of strength and are very attractive to females. This is why males have evolved to look so different from the females. When a male is sexually active, he puts on weight and his colours become more vibrant.

Forming Bonds

From the moment it is born, a monkey must learn to make friends and influence other members of its troop. Without friends, a monkey will get less food and have a harder time rearing its young. Grooming is the social glue that bonds monkey groups together. Monkeys groom each other while they are lazing around, waiting for their food to digest. Grooming is relaxing, and relaxed monkeys are less likely to get into fights. Instead, they work together to find food and raise their young.

Many prosimians use their body scent to avoid confrontations with others. The smells are a signal to other monkeys coming into its territory. Once everyone knows who is in charge in each area, the animals do not get into fights very often.

▲ MARKING A MESSAGE
A dominant male lemur marks a branch with a scent gland on his bottom. The other males in the band will smell wherever he's been and make sure they are friendly when they meet him.

◄ TUG OF LOVE
The mothering instinct has got the better of the young, inexperienced baboon on the right. She is snatching a baby from its mother. The baby will probably come to no harm, but baby-snatchers sometimes just abandon infants, who then have to be saved by their mums.

PATERNAL INSTINCTS ►
Everyone likes babies, and that's true for monkeys, too. Male monkeys are always jostling with each other for dominance. When an argument gets too much for one male, he may hold up a baby to his rival. Both males forget their disagreements and look after the infant.

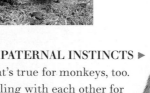

▲ SPIDER GROOMING SESSION

A spider monkey checks its friend's fur for lice and ticks. Spider monkeys are very social animals and live in big groups. When resting, these monkeys groom as many other monkeys as they can. If there are too many animals in the group for everyone to groom everyone else, the troop is too large, and the members split up into smaller groups.

▲ GIVING MUM A BREAK

The females in most monkey societies baby-sit for each other. A baby monkey may be suckled by several females as it grows. This tiny grey langur baby is being cared for by an aunty. Young female monkeys learn how to look after babies by caring for their relatives' young.

Did you know? Many monkeys spend almost half their days grooming each other.

HANDS UP FOR GROOMING ▶

A male chacma baboon grooms a female during a break from feeding. Males do a lot of grooming to make sure everyone in the troop likes them. When the breeding season arrives, the females that have enjoyed being groomed by a male will probably be happy to mate with him as well.

◀ LAID-BACK LANGUR

When a monkey is being groomed, its brain releases chemicals, called endorphins, that make the animal very relaxed. Relaxed monkeys are less stressed and will catch fewer diseases, give birth to more babies and be better at avoiding predators. Monkeys will groom even when they are clean and fresh.

A Hamadryas

Male hamadryas baboons are constantly posing threateningly to each other in attempts to win the right to mate with females. The baboons live in small groups known as harems, made up of a single male and several females. All the other males are constantly arguing and fighting to try to take control of another male's harem. The males are more fearsome looking than the females. They have long manes and dark red faces. Dominant males jealously guard their females, always herding them into a single group.

Hamadryas baboons have adapted to survive in near-desert conditions in Ethiopia and Somalia in Africa, and in southern Arabia on the other side of the Red Sea. They are smaller than other baboons, with brown rather than greyish coats.

TOGETHERNESS
A huddle of females keeps warm in the chilly desert night. The male is at the back on the right. At night, a troop of hundreds of hamadryas baboons may spend the night together for warmth and safety.

CLAN SOCIETY
A female hamadryas baboon rests on a rock. During the day, these monkeys spread out to look for food. The troop divides into smaller groups called clans. A clan is made up of the harems of several related males. Large troops contain two or three clans. Smaller troops have just one. The hamadryas community is the most orderly of all monkey societies.

Baboon Troop

SHOW OF POWER

This is not a yawn of tiredness, but a serious warning to other males not to get too close to this top baboon's harem. Male hamadryas are armed with powerful jaws and long teeth. The layout of their teeth means that the dagger-like canines rub against teeth in the lower jaw, and are kept good and sharp. Like its red face and silver mane, the baboon's teeth are a sign of power.

BANISHMENT

A young male baboon flees from its family group, chased away by its father. As soon as males are old and big enough to be a threat, the top male banishes them from his harem. The young males band together in twos and threes, and join forces to attack a harem in a bid to steal the females. Then they will fight each other for control. The losers of this battle are banished back to the bachelor life.

THE GENTLE SEX

Female hamadryas baboons do not get involved in fights. They spend their time being friendly. They look after the children and groom each other. Most harems have four or five females and their children, but there may sometimes just be a single female. Because they neither compete nor fight, the female baboons are much smaller than the males.

Mating Time

For all animals, mating is a fiercely competitive business. Males want to be sure that it is their genes, rather than those of any other male, that carry on to the next generation. Male monkeys and prosimians fight for the right to mate with females, and bring into play many different strategies to win their favour.

In rainforests, where there is a year-round food supply and the weather is always warm, the young can be cared for at any time of the year. The female primates that live there are able to breed throughout the year. For monkeys and prosimians that live in seasonal climates, however, there may be only one short period in the year when the females are ready to mate. The breeding season has to be timed so that when the young are born there will be plenty of food available and the weather is not too extreme.

▲ FEMALE CHOICE

Two red-bellied lemurs share a flower. The male on the left can be identified by the white patches under his eyes. Among tamarins, marmosets, capuchins and leaf-eating monkeys, it is the females who choose their mates. Tamarins and marmosets lick and cuddle their chosen mate. Capuchins flirt by raising their eyebrows, and leaf-eating monkeys pucker their lips invitingly.

◄ FIGHT FOR FEMALES

The colobus monkey on the left is the dominant male of his society. Only he has the right to mate with his group of females. The dominant monkey is attacking another male who has challenged him. Female colobus monkeys have a short breeding time, so the competition to claim a group of females is intense.

▲ ONCE A YEAR ONLY

Vervets live a comparatively tough life on the savanna. They have longer pregnancies than forest monkeys in the same family, so that the baby develops more in the safety of the womb. Once they are born, the babies have to grow up quickly so that they can learn to look after themselves and not be a burden on their parents.

▲ READY AND WAITING

A female black macaque is ready to breed. Her genitals have swollen into large, red, balloon-like pads. These swellings indicate to a male macaque that she may allow him to mate with her. Many female monkeys have a visual signal like this to show they are ready to mate. Prosimians advertise by scent and calling.

Nazca Monkey

The Nazca people lived in southern Peru about 2,000 years ago. They are famous because they produced a set of huge etchings 120 metres long in the deserts in that area. These etchings include pictures of animals, including one of a monkey. Nobody knows

why the Nazca people made these etchings, especially since the pictures cannot be seen from the ground. They were only discovered when an airplane flew over them.

▲ TILL DEATH DO US PART

A woolly lemur family huddles together affectionately in the Madagascan night. These lemurs form strong pair bonds. A male and a female mate only with each other throughout their lives. To keep in touch, they call to each other with long, high-pitched whistles.

Growing Up

Monkeys and lemurs spend a lot of time looking after their young – it is a way of giving them a better chance of survival. In many social groups, adults like to gather around babies. They may find food for the mother, and help look after the child. Langur mothers move away from their troop to give birth. They feed and bond with the baby before introducing it to its relations and friends. All this interaction means that the youngsters soon pick up communication skills. Baby monkeys call out to their mothers in high-pitched voices.

Most primates have only one baby at a time. Nocturnal prosimians tend to have shorter, more frequent pregnancies than monkeys and lemurs. The babies develop less in the womb but grow up quickly after birth. Bush babies start life in a nest, but by 9 months are mature enough to have babies of their own.

▲ CARING FATHER
Young saddleback tamarins hitch a lift from their father. Because tamarins and marmosets have two or three babies at a time, the fathers get involved in childcare. The children go back to their mother for feeding. Most monkeys only have one baby, which is carried by its mother.

◄ PLAY AND LEARN
Young chacma baboons play-fight together. They are learning how to use their growing bodies and practise pulling faces and making noises. They will use these tactics when they are older to threaten enemies or make friends. When young baboons are two or three months old, they start to explore away from their mothers.

◄ HEALTHY DRINK

Baby monkeys start suckling as soon as they are born. The infants of some leaf-eating species are not strong enough to eat solid food until they are 15 months old. Smaller species with more varied diets, such as marmosets, suckle their young for about two months. Lorises, which are nocturnal prosimians of South-east Asia, feed their babies infrequently but with very rich milk, to give the mothers more time to forage for food.

▲ BACHELOR BAND

Young hanuman langur males form gangs and wait for a chance to take over the troop. They have been chased away from the group by their father, the ruling male, because they are a threat to his leadership. In some primate societies that are controlled by a single male, a new leader may kill all the infants because he does not want to look after someone else's children. The females, deprived of their children, are soon ready to breed again and bear the new leader's children.

▲ LOOK AFTER ME!

Adult silver leaf monkeys of the Old World are looking after a couple of youngsters. Other members of a monkey troop may help a mother with childcare. The orange fur of the baby is a signal to the rest of the troop that they must treat the baby very gently. As the monkey grows up, its fur becomes grey and black, like its older friend on the right.

Did you know? Langur mothers hide their young high in trees to protect them from murdering males.

49

A Young Macaque

Female macaques are pregnant for about five months before giving birth. All the adult females in a troop become pregnant at the same time. The babies are born at the time of year when there is most food.

Although the troop is led by a single dominant male, female macaques each mate with several males. This way, when the babies are born, all the males think they might be their fathers, and everyone works together to look after them.

A young macaque spends most of its time playing with friends. It learns how to express its feelings, and can soon spot when a monkey is angry, happy or hurt. These social skills are essential for adult macaques.

1 The newborn baby, a few hours old, is suckled by his mother. She gave birth alone in the early hours of the morning and spent a few hours bonding with her child, before bringing the new baby back to meet her friends in the troop.

2 The growing macaque clings to his mother. She must feed a lot while she is suckling her baby, so she can make enough milk. Females lose up to one third of their body weight while they are producing milk.

3 Mother and child must follow the troop long distances each day. Now he is bigger, the baby rides all day on his mother's back. That's thirsty work for mum, and while she stops for a drink of water, her son takes a look around. He is just learning to walk, and stumbles and trips close to his mother while she takes a rest or feeds.

Matures

4 For several months the young macaque has taken nothing but his mother's milk. Now he is independent enough to begin to seek out his own food. By his first birthday, the young macaque knows where to find and how to recognize ripe and tasty food. He feeds himself, munching on nuts, fruits and plant shoots.

5 The young macaque is getting increasingly adventurous. Here he sets off to explore a watering hole. However, danger is all around, and he rarely strays far from his mother. Although she probably has a new baby by now, the young macaque will continue to live with his mother until he is four years old.

6 While still with his mother, the macaque begins to make friends with other monkeys. By grooming and being groomed, the young monkey takes his place in the troop. He learns which macaques are in charge, and, while under the watchful eye of his mother, he begins to get involved in the politics of the troop.

7 The macaque is now a fully grown male and he is less and less welcome in the troop. Soon he will have to leave home and set out to find another troop to join. He will need all his social and political skills to be accepted by them. Once in the new troop, he will have to spend a few years being kind to the females, and eventually they will let him father their children.

Monkey Relations

Prosimians, monkeys and apes are all members of the order of animals called primates. Each evolved in turn, adapting first to a life in the trees, and gradually relying on their intelligence to survive. Prosimians and less intelligent monkeys are called lesser primates. The advanced primates, or anthropoids (man-like), are the bigger-brained monkeys and apes. There are 19 ape species (compared with 242 species of monkey). Gibbons, known as the lesser apes, are the largest group and the most monkey-like. The great apes are gorillas, chimpanzees, orangutans, bonobos and humans. Of all primates, the great apes are the best at holding and manipulating small objects in their hands — and people are the most skilled of all.

KING OF SWING ▶

A lar gibbon swings through the forests of Asia. Gibbons are expert swingers, with arms as long as the rest of their body and legs together. Tails were not necessary for balance and so disappeared. Gibbons look for grubs on the ground, and have to raise their arms in the air to stop them dragging. Male and female gibbons live as a couple for life.

◀ KINDRED SPIRITS

The white back of this gorilla shows he is a full-grown male. Like people, older gorillas, especially males, get white hair. It's a sign of their strength and experience. Gorillas are the largest primates. They are around twice the weight of a well-built adult man, and over 2m tall. The animals live in permanent family groups in the forests of central Africa. Their senses of sight and hearing, and many of their gestures, are similar to ours.

TOO CLEVER BY HALF ▶

Like other apes, humans are descended from the primates that developed in the Old World. People are the most intelligent animals on Earth. As a result, humans can live in any environment. They can shape – and often destroy – the natural world to suit their needs. This young girl is only a few years older than the woolly monkey she is holding, but she has always been cleverer than the monkey.

▲ OLD MAN OF THE FOREST

The people of South-east Asia thought that orangutans were old men who had left their villages to live quietly in the trees. Orangutans are the world's largest tree-living animal, and have to climb slowly, choosing the strongest branches. They spend much of their time wandering alone through the forests looking for fruit.

◀ CLEVER PRIMATE

Bonobos are the closest ape relative to humans. They are the only other primate that regularly walks upright. Standing on two legs enables them to see over long distances, reach food on branches and have both arms free so that they can catch fish or hold their young.

▲ LESSONS WITH MOTHER

A chimpanzee baby is dependent on its mother for about five years. It has plenty of time to learn about how to behave in the complicated chimpanzee society. Chimps live in small patches of rainforest in central Africa. They form close relationships with each other and can make and use simple tools. They spend a lot of time on the ground, but climb trees to find fruit and to sleep.

Habitat Destruction

▲ TRIBAL PREDATORS
The traditional weapon of hunters in South American forests is a blow pipe. The hunters fire poisoned darts from the long pipe with a quick out-breath. The poison is a paste made from crushed plants or frog skins. In Africa, traditional hunters catch monkeys in nets, or fire arrows from a small bow.

MONKEY MEAL ▶
A man cooks a monkey in a central African forest. Traditional hunters do not kill more than they need for their families, so do not threaten the monkey populations. In some parts of the world, however, more and more people want to eat monkey meat. Hunters, armed with guns, kill monkeys for the bush meat trade. If the demand for monkey meat continues to increase, some areas may soon have no wild monkeys left at all.

Tribal peoples who live in the tropical rainforests and other wild habitats exist in harmony with monkeys and prosimians. They form part of the natural balance of their environment, along with the plants and other animals. The people take only what they need from their surroundings for building materials, food and medicines, and do not threaten the ecosystem.

On a global scale, though, humans are the world's dominant species and they exploit the Earth's resources for their own ends. They destroy habitats to make room for cities and roads, and for farmland to feed their huge populations. As a result, the habitats of many prosimian and monkey species are either chopped up into fragments too small to support them, or lost altogether. The animals then face extinction.

◄ DEFORESTATION

This barren, South American landscape was once thickly forested, and home to howler and black squirrel monkeys, and capuchins. The trees were cut and burned to make space for grazing cattle. The ash fertilizes the soil, briefly. Soon, though, without a rich variety of vegetation growing on it, the soil becomes poor and dusty. More forest is then destroyed to make new farmland.

LAST REFUGE ►

These Verreaux's sifaka lemurs are one of many species that are unique to Madagascar. All lemur species are in danger as people cut down vast tracts of forest, mainly for fuel. More than 14 lemur species are known to have become extinct since the humans began settling the island around 2,000 years ago.

▲ TALKING DESTRUCTION

Mobile phones contain a rare metal called tantalum. It is found in only a few places around the world, including central Africa. Here, where mandrills and mangabeys struggle for survival, people are fighting over control of the tantalum. The war has made it very hard to protect the monkeys.

◄ HIGHWAY ROBBERY

A lorry transports logs that have been cleared to make way for a road. Roads and villages in a forest can make it difficult for monkey populations to meet each other. Cut off from one another, they face extinction. Monkeys need to mate with other groups to produce healthy young. They also need to move easily to areas where there is food.

55

Life in a

Monkeys have lived alongside people throughout history. When humans began to farm and settle in communities, monkeys soon learned that there were easy pickings to be had. These monkeys were the generalist (non-specialist) species with a varied diet. Among them were the cheeky capuchins of the New World, the wily macaques of southern Asia and the highly adaptable vervets of Africa.

In many towns and cities there are monkey species that have been urbanized for generations. They have bigger and denser populations than any that exist in the wild.

EASY PICKINGS

A macaque's hands are ideal for foraging among human rubbish. Urban monkeys are clever and adaptable and will eat anything! They watch humans and learn where food supplies may be and how to get at them. They often take just a mouthful before moving on to the next readily available snack.

HUMAN TASTES

Like most urban monkeys, this vervet has developed a taste for human food. In some cities, urban monkeys have become pests and are bold enough to steal from shops and even food cupboards in houses. Tourists from countries where there are no monkeys are fascinated by them and feed them. This encourages the monkeys to scavenge even more.

Concrete Jungle

ALMS FOR THE POOR

In India, one monkey species has become known as the temple macaque, because large numbers of them live around temples. Often, rows of holy men and poor people begging line the roads to the temples. The monkeys have learned to beg, too – for scraps of food from the tourists and worshippers. One of the reasons why macaques and other urban monkeys fit so comfortably into city life is because human society is similar in many ways to how monkey groups live and interact.

ON THE ROCK

Barbary macaques live in Gibraltar, scavenging rubbish and food from tourists. They are the only monkeys to live wild in Europe. Barbary macaques are sometimes confused by the signals from people. They have been known to attack people who smile and stare, because these are aggressive signals in macaque society.

WHERE THERE'S A WILL...

City monkeys, especially vervets, steal food from people's homes. They can open doors, cupboards and boxes containing food. The vervets can be very determined, and will spend a lot of time working out a way to break in, and even brave a shock from an electric fence. People try to protect their homes by putting bars over windows, locking doors, or setting up alarms.

Use and Abuse

Humans have often woven magical stories around monkey characters and even worshipped monkey gods. However, they have also captured monkeys and used them cruelly.

By international law, it is illegal to buy and sell monkeys without a licence. This may be given, say, for the purposes of scientific experiments. Unfortunately, some animals are illegally exported, often travelling long distances in cramped and cruel conditions.

Many monkey and ape species are eaten in Africa and South-east Asia. Most are eaten by local people, for whom monkeys are a cheap source of "bush meat". However, more and more monkey meat is being smuggled around the world, especially into Europe and China, where it is sold illegally for very high prices. Conservationists believe that, if the bush meat trade is not stopped, many monkeys and apes could be wiped out within a few years.

▲ AT YOUR SERVICE
In Malaysia, macaques are trained to climb palm trees to pick coconuts. The agile monkeys easily scramble up to the top of the trees, where the coconuts grow. The macaques have learned to throw the coconuts down to their human owner. Although the monkeys are captive, this task is similar to the behaviour of wild macaques.

◄ PERFORMANCE
In parts of Asia, monkeys, such as this rhesus macaque, are trained to perform tricks to earn money for their human owners. Wild animals in captivity are often treated cruelly by being forced to perform in a way that is completely unnatural to them. Monkeys are not domesticated animals that have been bred to live with humans.

▲ OBEYING ORDERS

This monkey has been put in a cage to stop it escaping. The monkey will behave toward its human owner as a low-ranking male would do to a troop leader in the wild: it will cower to avoid confrontation and will try to do what the owner wants in return for access to food.

▲ FOR THE SAKE OF THE HUMAN RACE

Live monkeys are sometimes used in scientific experiments. This is called vivisection. Some of these monkeys are injured or killed. Many scientists believe that vivisection provides important information that could reduce the suffering of human beings, but others disagree.

◄ TAKE OFF!

A space shuttle blasts off. In the early days of space travel, many monkeys were used in experiments to study weightlessness.

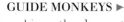

GUIDE MONKEYS ►

Capuchins – the cleverest New World monkeys – have been taught to help disabled people. The monkeys can pick up objects such as telephones and take them to their owners, as well as perform tasks such as operating switches. Although their owners might benefit, not everyone thinks that it is right to use monkeys in this way.

Saving Species

When the last member of a species dies, that species is extinct. It is lost forever. In the last few decades, some people have worked to stop the rarest primate species becoming extinct. Some have started sanctuaries and zoos where animals are helped to breed away from predators. Nearly half of the world's total population of aye-ayes (one of the most threatened lemurs in Madagascar) is in zoos because there is not enough of their natural habitat left to support them.

To save an endangered species, the cause of the threat must be addressed. This might be the destruction of the animal's habitat or the poverty of the people who hunt them. We can all affect the survival of species by making sure that we do not buy products that cause damage to a monkey's habitat.

▲ LIFE IN A COLD CLIMATE

Woolly monkeys come from the steamy jungles of Brazil. This one lives in English woodland. The monkeys' natural habitat in Brazil is being destroyed by humans and the species is disappearing fast. At their cliff-top home in the south-west of England, the monkeys are given special foods to make sure they get the same minerals in their diet as they would in the wild.

Did you know? Thanks to conservationists, only one primate has become extinct in 100 years.

◀ BACK TO THE WILD

Gerald Durrell, a British conservationist, holds a red-ruffed lemur. Durrell set up a pioneering zoo on the island of Jersey. Many rare primates have been bred there, and the zoo has successfully reintroduced lemurs and tamarins to their natural habitats. The Jersey zoo teaches keepers from other zoos how to raise captive-born animals so they can be released back into the wild.

◄ HOME FROM HOME

A rainforest has been created in New York's Bronx Zoo. The temperature, humidity and light are as close as possible to the natural conditions. Captive primates raised in a habitat similar to their wild environment are less likely to become distressed. They will stand a better chance of survival if they are later released into the wild.

KEEPING TRACK ►

These two golden lion tamarins, born in a zoo, were released into a protected area of Brazilian forest. Scientists fitted them with radio transmitters to keep track of them. This species has been saved from extinction by being bred in zoos around the world.

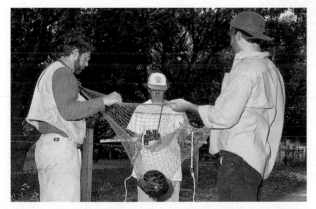

▲ ONE IN THE BAG

Scientists have shot a howler monkey with a drugged dart. They will take some measurements then give the monkey another drug to bring it back to consciousness. Their aim is to gain as much information as possible about the howler monkey's population make-up, its diet and the diseases it suffers. This will help them to understand how to conserve the species better.

▲ SAFE SANCTUARY

A monkey whose parents were killed by hunters has been rescued and taken to an orphanage. Sometimes, young monkeys that were captured illegally are rescued and sent to zoos to be cared for. They can't be set free as they don't know how to survive in the wild.

GLOSSARY

agile
Moving quickly and easily.

ape
A large, tailless primate with long arms. Chimpanzees, gorillas, gibbons, orangutans, bonobos and humans are all apes.

band
A group of prosimians, such as ring-tailed lemurs, similar to a troop of monkeys.

carcass
The dead body of an animal.

clan
A subgroup of a troop of hamadryas baboons, made up of three of four related male baboons and their harems of females.

diet
The food an animal eats.

digit
A finger, thumb or toe.

dominant
A monkey or prosimian that is in charge of, or is dominant in a troop or band.

ecosystem
A group of living things in a certain area that live together and interact with and depend on each other.

endorphin
A chemical produced by the brain that gives an animal a relaxed, contented feeling.

extinct
When every member of a species of animal or plant is dead.

fermentation
A chemical process that breaks down sugars and starches. Fermentation occurs in the stomachs of animals that eat a lot of plants.

fovea
A patch of highly sensitive cells at the centre of a retina in the eye. Forveas help monkeys to see very clearly.

generalist
An animal that eats all types of food.

gharial
A small type of crocodile found in Asia.

grooming
When monkeys clean each other's fur.

harem
A group of females that is controlled by a single male.

home range
An area of land or territory that generally takes an animal or group of animals several weeks or months to move through.

Jacobson's organ
A small organ at the top of many animals' mouths that helps them to detect smells better. Many prosimians have these organs.

keratin
The protein used to make hair and fingernails.

leader
The monkey or prosimian in charge of the troop, band or harem. Not all primate societies have leaders.

mammal
A hairy animal that feeds its young on milk.

mangrove
A type of tropical tree that grows close to water. Mangrove roots hang down from the plant into the water.

mineral
A type of chemical that is given in food and is essential for good health.

New World
The name given to North and South America. Monkeys from the New World usually have prehensile tails and flat noses with outward-facing nostrils.

niche
The position a species takes in an ecosystem. It may refer to an animal's diet or the time of day it eats.

nutrient
A part of food that gives an animal energy and good health.

Old World
The name given to Europe, Asia and Africa. Monkeys and prosimians from the Old World usually have tails for balance and small noses with downward-facing nostrils.

opposing thumb
A thumb that is 'opposite' the fingers, like a human thumb. Opposing thumbs help a primate to pick up small objects.

orbit
The circular part of an animal's skull that holds the eye.

pollen
The male sex cell of a plant, produced by flowers.

prehensile
A part of the body that is adapted for grasping and gripping. Many monkeys and other mammals have prehensile tails.

primate
A group of mammals, to which prosimians, monkeys and apes belong. All primates have forward-facing eyes and flexible hands.

proboscis
A long, flexible nose, such as that of the proboscis monkey.

prosimian
A primitive type of primate, such as a lemur or bush baby.

protein
A type of nutrient used to make muscles and other structures in an animal's body.

quadruped
An animal that walks on four legs.

rhinarium
The moist area on some animals' noses that joins the nostrils to the lips. It enhances an animal's sense of smell.

savanna
Tropical grassland that has only a few trees. Most savanna is in Africa.

skeleton
A framework of bones inside an animal's body, giving it support and strength.

social animal
An animal that lives in a group.

solitary animal
An animal that lives alone.

species
A group of animals that can breed with each other and share many similar features. Two animals from diffeent species cannot mate with each other.

territory
The area that an animal or group of animals lives in and defends from others.

troop
The name given to a group of monkeys.

venom
Natural poison produced by some reptiles, insects and other animals. these animals use venom to kill their prey and to defend themselves from attackers.

Picture Acknowledgements

Ardea: 49 tr/P Steyn: 5 tr, 15 tr, 22 tl, 56 br/ A and E Bomford: 8 br/M Watson: 9 c / F Gohier: 10 c, 23 tr, 36 br/C Haagner: 21 cl/ J-P Ferrero: 25 tr, 25 b, 32 cl, 42 cl, 42 br/ B Osborne: 22 bl/N Gordon: 28 tl/P Morris: 29 cr, 39 br/K Lucas: 34 bl/Ferrero-Labat: 35 tl/K W Fink: 45 bl /A Warren: 53 cr/D Lasta: 55 bl/LR Beames: 56 tl/J Cancalosi: 57 cl; **BBC NH Unit**/P Oxford: 7 tl, 11 cl, 30 tl, 47 br, 48 tl, 58 bl/L M Stone: 9 bl/N Gordon: 10 tr, 26 br/D Wechsler: 13 cl/E D Ferrera: 18 tl, 18 bl, 19 cr, 19 b/A Shah: 19 tl, 21 tl, 26 bl, 27 tr, 33 tr, 40 br, 47 tr/S Widstrand: 30 bl/ M Wilkes: 31 tl/T Martin: 31 bl/P Savoie: 32 br/E A Kuttapan: 35 tr/I Arndt: 37 bl/B Walton: 40 bl, 41 tr/T Weald: 49 tl/D Shale: 50 br/B Castelein: 51 tl/B Davidson: 52 bl/ B Britton: 57 bl; **BBC Wild**/ C Taylor: 38 tl/ A Shah: 46 bl, 47 tl; **Biophotos**/B Rogers: 55 tl;

B Coleman/W Layer: 15 tl/J and P Wegner: 16 tr, 34 tr/B Coleman: 17 tl/S C Kaufman: 24 bl/ G Ziesler: 29 tr/R Magnusson: 36 tr/P van Gaalen: 44 tl; **Corbis Images**/D A Northcott: 44br/ W Kaehler: 55 cr/A Griffiths Belt: 59b/ C and A Purcell 61 br; E/G Neden: 5 bl; Heather Angel: 20 bl, 26 tr, 27 cr; **Hutchinson Library**/HR Dorig: 20 br; **Monkey Sanctuary**/ R Helvesi: 53 tr, 60 tl; **Nat History NZ Ltd**: 21 tr; **Naturepl**/A Shah: 42 cl/R du Toit: 43 cr/ I Arndt: 43 bl/K Bass: 53bl/N Lucas: 55 br; **NHPA**/N Garbutt: 4 tr/D Heuclin: 5 c, 17 br/ P German: 7 br/K Schafer: 13 tr, 37 tl/ T Kitchin and V Hurst: 14 tl/G Lacz: 15 b/ J Warwick: 23 tl/M Bowler: 23 br/A Rouse: 24 br/O Press: 25 tl/M Bowler: 38 br/P Fagot: 51 cl/M Harvey: 61 tl; **OSF**/D Haring: 5 tr, 13 br, 20 tr, 21br, 42 tr, 46 tr/M Deeble and V Stone: 6 tl/M W Richards: 7 c/M Leach: 9 tr/Z Leszczynski: 10 br, 28 bl, 39 cl, 39 c/ C Bromhall: 11 tr/M Colbeck: 11 tr, 18 br/ H Pooley: 11 br/L L T Rhodes: 14 bc/D Curl: 16 bl/S Breeden: 17 cl, 39 tl/K Lucas: 20 cr/ K Wothe: 23 cl/E Hashimoto: 24 tl/J Chellman: 27 bl/P Franklin: 29 tl/B Wright: 31 cr, 39 cr, 43 tr, 50 tl 51 br/R Davies: 32 tl/P Productions Ltd: 33 cl/M Kavanagh: 33 b/S Osolinski: 35 br, 40 tl/P J DeVries: 43 tl/B and B Wells: 45 tl/ B Kenney: 45 cr, 52 tl, 61 cr/J Sierra: 48 bl/ M Powles: 50 bl/D Tipling: 51 tr D J Cox: 53 tl/R Davies: 58a tr/D Cayless: 59/C Tyler: 60 br/M Tandy: 61c bl; P Pics/J Mills: 54 tl/ N Robinson: 54 br; **S American Pictures**/ T Morrison: 47 bl; **SPL**/N Dennis: 8 tl/ T Davis: 12 tr/T McHugh: 14 cr/ M Phillips: 41 cl/G C Kelley: 41 br/A Wolfe: 49 bl/NASA: 59 bl/ R Nannini: 59 br

INDEX